FOREWORD

"Make me an echo
Of the One I worship"

"The Spirit's encounter is holy surprise
……the mystic's enjoyment of fun."

Here, in Rosemary Radley's collection of poems, from "Semana Santa" to "An Epiphany", there are moments of insight, moments of surprise, moments of gratitude.

How lovely that an Anglican lay-woman wants to share something of her Grace of Gratitude.

Take these poems in small meditative moments - here a line, there a line – and unlooked-for treasures will be revealed.

The Very Reverend Dr Victor Stock, OAM

Advent Sunday
2nd December 2018

INTRODUCTION

It was difficult to know how to present my poems for this book. Some are ancient and others are modern; some are only a few lines, others are long. I have to admit, several are very long, but I hope, not boring!

My decision to put them in chronological order has had its problems. It has been difficult to give an accurate date to the longer poems their very length inevitably, meant they took longer to complete.

Mostly, my poetry is devotional, with two or three otherwise! I trust that their inclusion is not disturbing.

I take this opportunity to thank Father Victor Stock for kindly agreeing to write a Foreword to my collection of poetry. I reminded him recently of the occasion of our first cursoy meeting at 6 Gower Street, Bloomsbury, when I was secretary to Fr Gordon Phillips, Head of the Anglican Chaplaincy to the University of London. Both Fr Victor and I held up our hands in horror, metaphorically-speaking, "That was sixty years ago!" he exclaimed.

Also, I thank Gordon Drayson who has assembled my poems in book form and prepared them for publication at Erlanger Press.

Rosemary Elisabeth Radley

Rosemary, when she was happy
- in Blackheath

CONTENTS

INTRODUCTION	4
A CHRISTMAS MEDITATION	7
THE COMPASSIONATE CHRIST	8
OFFERTORY	9
MINE INHERITANCE	10
WHITE MARTYRDOM	11
THE GAIETY OF GOD	12
SILENT EUCHARIST	13
SEMANA SANTA	14
THE ROSE	17
UNION WITH GOD	18
LA BELLE HELENE	19
THE GRACE OF GRATITUDE	22
THE DIVINE HUMILITY	23
A MYSTIC'S NOVICIATE	24
A BEAUTIFUL FLOWER	25
AN ICON OF CHRIST?	26
CHE SERIAH, SERIAH	27
THE PEOPLE OF GOD TRAVEL TO VICTORY/VICTORIA	28
EASTER MORN IN MEDIEVAL LONDON	30
SUFFERING GLORY	34
AVILA, OH AVILA!	36
THE HOLY FACE	37
THRICE HOLY GOD	38
CLOSE TO THE HEART OF GOD	40
BECOMING IS BEAUTIFUL	41
AN EPIPHANY!	42
A MYSTICAL DAY	43
BREAD OF ANGELS	45

A CHRISTMAS MEDITATION

As darkness falls on Bethlehem, the waiting world is still
Angels glorify the Lord to shepherds on the hill;
They bring Good News from heaven to everyone on earth,
Telling of the manger and the Saviour's humble birth:
"Arise, and come to Jesus," the angelic voices sing,
"Fall down and adore the Christ, who's born to be your King."
And when the heavenly host had gone the shepherds were away
Hastening to Bethlehem to where the Christ child lay.

Within a humble stable they find the living Light
Radiantly shining to illuminate the night.
Adoringly, the holy angels hover o'er the place
Hallowed by the Saviour Christ and Mary full of grace.
Here Jesus, son of Mary, is laid upon a stall,
Worshipped by the shepherds, acknowledged Lord of all.
Encircled by the ass and oxen welcoming their guest,
Jesus smiles upon his mother, Mary ever blest.
"Behold, the Son of God", she cries, and great is Mary's joy -
Joy that no discomfort of the stable can destroy,

Devoted in her love for Jesus, constant in her gaze,
Mary magnifies the Lord with undivided praise.
Here faithful Joseph watches o'er the Virgin with her Child,
While Mary's soul rejoices, her spirit undefiled.
In contemplation of God's love does Mary ever dwell,
By love, it was that she conceived the Christ, Emmanuel.
She offers up th' incarnate Word with heartfelt adoration,
Grateful to their Father for the fruit of her vocation.

1962

THE COMPASSIONATE CHRIST

The Spirit of the Lord
Rests upon us
To bless
Our impoverished life
With the charism of Love,
Compassionate, Sacrificial.

By the grace of our Father God
His compassion dwells within:
He is the divine replenisher
Of our empty vessels,
Embalming our needy humanity,
Sharing his healing divinity;
Tending the wounded soul.
Letting his *agape* dwell within us,
Offering succour to the poor,
And solace to the desolate:
Drawing one human soul
Closer to another;
Christ the compassionate.

Merciful Lord Jesus Christ;
We are humbled
By your Death on the Cross
And your Resurrection Life.
Embalm our fallen humanity
And bind up the broken heart,
Christ, the compassionate.
By your Grace, equip us
To show compassion to the other.

Heavenly Father,
We give you praise and thanksgiving
For the Gift of your Holy Spirit
That we might know how to love
The unloved and the unlovely.
In truth, what if we,
Who boldly claim to be
The Body of Christ on earth,
Lack the Love of Christ the compassionate?

1975

Agape, Greek for Christian spiritual love.

OFFERTORY

O, Lord, of the Transfiguration,
Honour my humble oblation,
Sanctify, hallow and bless
The off'ring of all I possess.
I am not rightfully mine,
All that I am, Lord, be thine;
Burn out each sinful desire
With the flame of thy Holy Ghost fire.
Wilful self-seeking efface
By the transforming power of thy grace,
That through me thy glory may shine
And the human be rendered divine;
I consecrate self unto thee,
Lord, I pray thee to transfigure me.

1984

MINE INHERITANCE

Take heed, O my soul:

Walk the way thy Lord has trod,
Be still, and know that I am God.
Dwell in him, that he might be
Forevermore indwelt with thee.
Thou art privileged in Christ
To whom thy life be sacrificed;
To whose poverty submit thy spirit,
That thou eternal life inherit.
And do not let thy sin profane
The stamp of Love thou wouldst attain.
Seek after God, love is the key,
Attired in Christ's humility.
And in his mercy the Lord will bless
Thee, O soul, with holiness;
Enrichment of thine impoverished state
The Spirit will be incarnate.
How shall I joy when thou embrace
The full benediction of his Grace.

1985

WHITE MARTYRDOM

I would be beautiful, Father, for thee,
An intrepid witness to Love's design;
In the power of the Spirit beautify me,
As unto the crucified Christ I incline.
Becoming is beautiful, transform me within,
Make me a spiritual sacrifice,
Dead to the world, to self and to sin,
Enduring reproach to honour Love's price.
The call of the Cross I cannot resist;
Yet shall I abide when I suffer loss?
Obedience be mine if I'm to persist
Along the royal road of the Holy Cross.
A life-long oblation perfected through prayer,
Sustained by the Spirit's life giving breath,
To serve the dark world whose sufferings I share,
A sign of the Cross, prepared unto death.
    Beautiful for God would I be,
    Gracious Jesus, beautify me.

1986

THE GAIETY OF GOD

A gladdening gift, the gift of gaiety,
A dance of delight with the living Lord,
Rapt by the kiss of the incarnate Deity,
His heart and mine secured by Love's cord,
With gayful abandon shall I realise
The blissful embrace of the ineffable Son;
The Spirit's encounter is holy surprise,
Source of the mystic's enjoyment of fun.
With a lilt in my spirit, a song in my heart,
The unalloyed music of heaven I'd capture;
In the chorus divine I'd joy to take part,
Ecstatic, my spirit transported in rapture.
Unto the heavenly banquet I'd climb.
As the Spirit of Love, my spirit enchants,
Leading me into God's presence sublime,
Fulfilled by the grace of th' eternal dance.
The Spirit within, the Spirit without,
How I shall marvel at Christ's courtesy,
My praises mingled with the saints' all about
That mystical fellowship encompassing me.
    Oh, that I were my Lord's delight,
    An offering worthy in his sight.

1988

SILENT EUCHARIST

Lord,
For the silence of this hour
In the silence of the night
Affording silence to my soul,
I make eucharist
On the alter of my heart,
That my life become
A complete offering,
A perfect oblation
And grant me the Grace of Gratitude
Unto God,
In the Name of the Trinity,
Father,
Son
And Holy Spirit.
Amen

1989

SEMANA SANTA
Holy Week in Sevillia

Tonight, in the byways of ancient Seville
Scent from the orange groves wafts where it will.
The quaint cobbled *calles* weave uphill and down,
Narrow and twisting, entwining the town.
Closely-wedged houses grace old thoroughfares,
Huddled, in contrast to grand spacious squares.
Within every courtyard as pilgrims pass by,
Picturesque *patios* capture the eye.

The evening is still, the atmosphere warm,
When into the heart of *Sevillia* folk swarm;
They congregate densely, each jostling the other,
Eager to welcome the heavenly Mother.
Black-hooded penitents, sparingly shod,
Offer devotion to the Mother of God.

There's hope in the distance, as a dazzling light
Pierces its way through the dark of the night.
With dignified splendour, *el paseo* draws near:
La Senora sangradissima is about to appear
Adorned with a mantle of delicate lace,
As white as a snowdrop, as pure as her face;
Encrusted with jewels, her shimmering train
Falls like a shower of glistening rain.
Clouds of sweet incense encompass *Madonna*,
Its heavenly fragrance enhancing her honour.
The candlelit *paseo* precariously sways,
Decked with magnificent floral bouquets.
The faithful rejoice to behold the procession,
Praying the Virgin to make intercession.
Our Lady is borne through a jubilant crowd,
Elating the humble, subduing the proud.

"*Maria, bellissima!*" they lovingly cry
To the most favoured woman who passes closeby.
They wave from the doorways, they wave from the road,
Gaily they wave from each humble abode.
They crowd onto balconies, never to miss
The chance to blow Mary their tenderest kiss.
But some hover sadly and invoke Mary's prayer,
Seeking her succour and motherly care.

A cripple pleads urgently, so heavy his cross:
"*Maria! carissima Ore por nostros*",
An ancient senora appeals through her gaze:
"*Recuerdese de mi, querida*", she prays.
Her bitterness melts after ages of trial,
Warmed at the sight of Our Lady's sweet smile,
Mary's virginal face has a radiant glow,
Lit by the clusters of candles below:
Eager, yet patient, folk love to surround
Maria sangradissima, whom Jesus has crowned.
Her ardent admirers gaze up to behold
The Mother of Christ with a crown of pure gold.
Feint hearts are kindled, the poor are serene;
They welcome their Mother and fête her as Queen.

But look! The great *paseo* stops with a lurch
Near to the entrance of *Santa Cruz* church.
El padre is prostrate, he's humble indeed,
Telling the Virgin his every need,
When, from under the float, with a laugh and a shout,
Hot sweaty faces peer jovially out;
A chorus of *"Bravos"* surprises the seers -
And a flask of *Cinzano* from nowhere appears,
A swig is most welcome, a-moistening the lips,
Quenching the thirst of each bearer that sips.

None would deny the real honour assured,
Lightening the burden steadfastly endured,
Yet a breath of fresh air is a welcome relief
From the weight to be borne – tho' the respite is brief.

The signal is given, the bearers recoil
Under the float to continue their toil:
Concerted in spirit, with a breathtaking heave
They lift high the *paseo* before taking leave:
With a list to the left, and a list to the right,
Once more, Our Lady proceeds through the night.

Sevillia 1970

Footnote
Semana Santa	*Holy Week*
Calles	*Lanes*
El paseo	*The Float*
Santa Cruz	*Holy Cross*
Ore pro nostros	*Pray for us*
Recuerdes mi, querida	*Remember me, beloved*
Carissima	*Very lovely*
Sangradissima	*Lady most holy*
La Senora Bellissima	*Lady most beautiful*

N.B. *Written in 1970 after witnessing Semana Santa (Holy Week) in 1966, Roman Catholic Sevillia Spain, describing one of the many floats carried along the streets of Sevillia, and some possible exotic responses of the Spanish onlookers.*

THE ROSE

Mam'selle, a rose,
A rose without a thorn,
Plucked from out the hedgerow dew
Upon this summer morn.

Mam'selle, take heed
I prithee pour no scorn
Upon the fragrant rose I hold,
So diligently borne.

Mam'selle, a rose
My fairest to adorn,
Picked especially for thee,
To whom my love is sworn.

Mam'selle, 'tis I,
My heart is e'er forlorn,
Accept from me this perfect rose,
My Rose without a thorn.

1985

There was nothing personal involved with the above poem!
I composed it for its own sake.

UNION WITH GOD

Most glorious Holy Trinity
In your mercy I confide
To raise my sights to your perfection
Transcending transitory affection
But shall I last if I abide
Within your unity?

Oh! that my soul might enter in
To union divine;
To plumb the depths, to soar yet higher,
And find in God my heart's desire;
Oh! fire of love, my life refine,
Erase my every sin.

For mystical communion,
I ask, but do I dare?
To dwell in God my self must die;
I live, and yet it is not I,
Oh! Christ whose perfect life I bear,
Restore our broken union.

Despite the toil, the agony,
My hope is in my quest
That your presence will not let me go,
And even in this while below,
What bliss to bide among the blest,
To suffer joyful ecstasy.

1988

LA BELLE HELENE

Among the vines of Beaujolais whence flows the ruby wine,
Hélène, a humble peasant girl, felt called by Love divine.
She held a secret in her heart, confided to a few:
The priest, her mother and a friend; no other person knew.
Her village home knew poverty, the darkened rooms lay bare,
And ever since *Papa* had died she'd lived on bread and prayer.
Her mother was a lonely soul - *Hélène* was all she had;
She'd laboured hard in better days to keep her daughter clad.
Hélène adored *sa chère Maman*, her happiness was dear,
This call from God bewildered her, its wherefore was unclear.
With peace regaled, by joy fulfilled - with love, *Hélène* was ravished;
She prayed to know the Will of God, such were the blessings lavished.

The village youths, they fancied her, cried out, *"La belle Hélène!"*
But she was not enamoured of these passionate young men.
The sultry midday sun blazed down, no cloud despoiled the sky;
The bustling buyers raised the dust; their fervour made her sigh:
Le bavardant offended, *le marchandant* dismayed
The vision of *la belle Hélène*, the Spirit-filled young maid.
She groaned a groan she so abhorred the women's idle chatter,
De *"François et sa femme fatale"*, and other trivial matter.
Alone, *Hélène* would tend the vines, and praise the Lord in song;
She had no wish to entertain the village gossip-throng.

Hélène embraced the Saviour's Passion and shared His Agony;
She pondered hard His sufferings in dark Gethsemane.
La desolée was near despair, for deep was her Dark Night,
By naked faith she wrestled with the darkness of the Light.
In prayer to discern the Will of God, *Hélène* pursued her quest:
To emulate the Living Lord who was, by grace, her Guest.
The importunate cried out in vain, her pleading came to nought;
She wondered if she'd ever find the sanctuary she sought.

Confusion reigned within her heart about her true vocation.
For here she was, entranced, absorbed in contemplation;
Her fervent love for God ran deep, as did her heart's desire.
What was the longing of her soul? To what did she aspire?

She prayed the Holy Spirit to transform her humanity,
Yearning for the cloister's peace yet feared it couldn't be.
"Mon cher Seigneur," Hélène exclaimed *"tu as retiré moi!"*
Les souffrances de mon e sont tellement mon croix.
Je te remercie, cher Jesus, que je partage en ton Esprit,
Oh, montres-moi le vœu de Dieu et guide ma pauvre vie."
The torrid midday sun beat down, its brilliance seemed to mock
The sorrows of *la belle Hélène* of humble peasant stock,

When o'er the sated, scuffling crowd the *Angelus* rang clear;
Hélène fell down on well-worn knees, th' Almighty to revere,
She daily praised the Holy Spirit for Mary's life on earth,
For Mary's faithful *"Oui" à Dieu*, making possible Jesus' Birth.

Few in the market paused from work, for a little while, at least:
And the gossips ever gossiped, and the bustle never ceased,
The last bell tolled, *Hélène* arose, determined she would go
To tell *Monsieur le curé* of the call that vexed her so.
A man of God, a priest of prayer, whose church, *St Etienne*,
Was a place of prayer for village folk, especially *Hélène*!
The *curé* was a spiritual guide, confessor, pastor, friend:
Who, when he heard a heart-rending tale, a compassionate ear he'd bend.
She hastened to *le curé's* house, *l'ancien presbytère.*
"Bonjour, Hélène," le curé cried, *"Tout va bien, j'espère."*
Her solemn look and reddened eyes, belied a troubled heart,
Sharing in the suff'ring of the Saviour's Sacred Heart.
She raised her eyes and faintly smiled, her anguish he discerned.
Hélène poured forth the conflict that troubled and concerned.

"Dieu m'appelle vers lui, mon père; souvent, j'entends la voix.
Je n'peux répondre parce que ma mère a besoin de moi.
Toujours elle est alitée; elle reste sans visiteurs;
Papa était un communiste, et de Maman les gens ont peur.
Vraiment, Maman est ennuyée, sa foi n'existe plus.
Vous savez que son âme est sombre sans la présence de Jésus.

Ma mère paraît si oubliée, elle a un air si trist';
Son vivant charme a disparu, elle doute de l'amour de Christ.
Quand je lui parle de cet appel elle ouvr' à moi le cœur":
'Reste à la maison, ma mignonne; comprends ma grande douleur:
Ma fille, regardes ta mère toute seule, je deviens vieille.
Ma chère Hélène, si tu me quittes, ta Maman s'en mourrai.'"

"J'explique que Dieu est devenu le centre de ma vie;
Que Dieu m'a donné son amour et la joie du paradis.
J'assure Maman que je l'adore, que son bonheur m'est cher,
Mais toujours Dieu m'appelle vers lui! Mon père, que puis-je faire?
L'appel de Dieu m'emporte du monde et dechire ma loyauté.
Comprenez, s'il vous plaît, mon père, un esprit affligé.
Je veux remplir le vœu de Dieu, mais quel est son plaisir?
Oh, aidez-moi à savoir lequel le Dieu desire."
Compassion filled *the curé's* heart for all *Hélène* related;
He entered into the suff'ring with which her life was fated:
"Ma chère enfante, je comprends bien la souffrance de ton âme,
Mais pries en foi toujours, Hélène, Dieu restaura le calme.
Que le bon Seigneur t'a appellée je reste toujours très sûr;
Mais penses quand même à ta chère Maman, sa vie est déjà dure.

Le diable essaie de tromper tous ceux qui adorent Dieu;
Ne succombes pas à ses desseins; il n'aime pas les pieux.
Réjètes les oeuvres du diable, n'écoutes pas ce qu'il dit:
Ma fille, tu sais que Dieu est juste. Sois donc, Hélène, comme lui."

Late 1980s

THE GRACE OF GRATITUDE

O, gratitude, your grace be mine
To radiate the Lord's new wine;
By Christ's dear Passion we're fulfilled
By peace and joy with love distilled,
And so in eucharist we pray,
To offer gratitude each day.
In Christ's real presence we repent
And share the saints' entitlement:
Forgiveness from our blessed Lord,
A pure baptismal robe restored.

Now drunk with the Spirit from the cup
An inebriate heart we offer up
To the Father who honours Baptism's seal
Conferred on souls to save and heal.
The Holy Ghost I scarce contain,
His gifts of grace descend as rain.
What love o'erflows this inadequate flask,
Whose overflowing compels me ask:
Can the Spirit's Baptism be endued
Without the grace of gratitude?

1980

THE DIVINE HUMILITY

All praise to our Father
In Heaven,

All glory be
To Jesus Christ's humility.

Holy Spirit of God
Breath of Life,
Thee, I inspire,
I must expire.

But how can I inspire the Spirit,
I who am of little merit,
Since it is He
Who inspires me?

Praised be God's humility.

1986

A MYSTIC'S NOVICIATE

Convert me, O God, till my spirit conform
Perfectly unto thine;
Christ's wounds I embrace, O Father, transform
My soul unto Union divine.
Wound the proud heart with the stab of the Cross,
The crux of the mystic's call;
With the nails tool my life, the spirit emboss,
A victim of Love's enthral.

Bankrupt of spirit, the Dark Night afflicts,
No Spirit do I incarnate;
'Tis only the Love-filled life that depicts
A fruitful noviciate.
Invest me with Love, despite my discredit,
In the depths of my heart convene
A secret encounter of spirit with Spirit,
Ineffable Lover, unseen.

Fulfil me, O God, for the Kingdom I seek,
And the glory I hardly deserve,
Prepare me to go through the gateway unique
To the Belovèd's own preserve.
Dying to sin, the self mortified,
The grace of the Spirit to house;
Find nothing in me, save Christ crucified,
The bridegroom I pray to espouse.

Anoint me, O Spirit, confirm my endeavour
With Love, the charism sought.
In grace I would grow, my deal with sin sever,
That the Christ within me be wrought.
Silenced and stilled by the Spirit's power
I "sleep" in the deepest reflection:

Union with God is the prayer of the hour
To mirror the Saviour's perfection.

1988

A BEAUTIFUL FLOWER

Come unto the Lord,
Receive his embrace,
Lift up your heart
To the source of all grace.
When you stand in his Presence
In the quiet of the hour,
Pray that your soul
Will unfold like a flower.

Abandon your self
To God's every demand:
His Will, it is sovereign,
His Word is command.
When humbled before him
Beseech him to shower
Your soul with his grace,
As a dew-sprinkled flower.

You are God's glory,
His glory is yours,
All spiritual gifts
He gladly outpours.
When your heart is surrendered
To his sanctifying power
Your soul will unfold
Like a beautiful flower.

1989

AN ICON OF CHRIST?

Refining Fire of God
I would that I might be
Inexorably purged
And rendered whole by thee.
To be as thou art, pure,
Thy trials must be mine.
Lead me through the wilderness
My spirit to refine.

Transformed as pure gold,
Without the dross of sin,
May the likeness of our Saviour
Be conformed within.
Circumcise my spirit,
My inner self perfect;
An icon of the Christ I'd be
His radiance reflect.

In Christ my life is hid
And would that I might be
Transparent in his Presence
Bereft of secrecy.
No deception can I suffer,
No dark recesses hide;
O, would my disingenuous heart
Were wholly crucified.

His Kingdom dwells within,
The spirit is innate
Guided by the Holy Spirit
Through the narrow gate
Into the sanctum of my being
To discover God, and be

An icon of the living Christ
And his epiphany.

1988

CHE SERIAH, SERIAH
(Pronounced like the 'iah' of Uriah. Seriah was the name of my doctor)

Verse: When I was ill at Denmark Hill,
I asked Seriah, What can it be?
Will I get better, or will I get worse?
That's up to you, not me.

Chorus: *Che Seriah, Seriah,
Whatever will be, will be.
My future's at stake, you see.
Che Seriah, Seriah,
What will be, will be!*

Now that I'm feeling so much worse,
I ask, Seriah, What can it be?
Can I be cured, or am I a clot?
Seriah, please answer me.

Chorus: *Che Seriah, Seriah...*

Thank you, Seriah, for all you've done,
Thank you for saying what it might be.
Now that AEG burst open my head
And almost murdered me!

Chorus: *Che Seriah, Seriah...*

1957 - Obviously, I hadn't lost my sense of humour!

THE PEOPLE OF GOD TRAVEL TO VICTORY/VICTORIA
On the CLAPHAM OMNIBUS

                God made us man and woman,
                To mirror his perfection,
                That all of God's creation
                Might see the divine reflection.

Refrain: *Con anima et animus....*
                We come to God in omnibus.

                But man and woman'd turned away
                From God and all he'd planned:
                They had eaten of forbidden fruit,
                And from Paradise were banned

                Con anima et animus....

                The human race had fallen
                To a state without God's grace,
                Slowly, surely, to be restored,
                For all creation to see his face.

                Con anima et animus....

                We travel with the saints of God
                Singing "Deo Gloria",
                Rubbing shoulders with the world,
                From Clapham to Victoria.

                Con anima et animus....

August 1989

Footnote for On the Clapham Omnibus

Not the sort of poem I'd imagined I would write on a retreat at Pleshey, near Chelmsford, Essex, of Evelyn Underhill, Anglican Christian mystic and writer, fame, who made Pleshey her spiritual base for retreat-giving, between the Two World Wars.

N.B. The man on the Clapham Omnibus is a hypothetical ordinary and reasonable person, now used by the courts in English law where it is necessary to decide whether a party has acted as a reasonable person would, for example in a civil action for negligence. The man on the Clapham Omnibus is a reasonably educated, intelligent but non-descript person, against whom the defendant's conduct can be measured.

The term was introduced into English law during the Victorian era, and still is an important concept in British law. It is also used in other Commonwealth common law jurisdictions.

The route of the original London "Clapham Omnibus" is unknown, but route 88 is sometimes associated with the term, having been briefly branded in the 1990s as "The Clapham Omnibus".

It is apt that the terminus of the No. 88 bus is "Victoria"!

EASTER MORN IN MEDIEVAL LONDON

Lent's solemnities are past, the penitent is shriven,
The feckless make their peace with God, their every sin forgiven.
Friday was the day called Good, a day of prayer and fasting,
Today, the joy of Resurrection brings Life that's everlasting.
Come, join the Festal Day parade with heartfelt celebration;
Sing forth the Truth of Christendom with joyful jubilation.
Hark, the bells from Paul's cathedral peal that all might know
That Jesus Christ is Risen today, as did the Maudlin, long ago.
Ringers ring the changes, the City walls vibrate,
The faithful folk of London Town bring glory to the Fête.

Guillaume, gallant warrior, a handsome *fier* knight;
Embraces Brother Barnabas, the silent Carmelite.
Pious little Ethelburga tries to emulate
The saint, whose tiny church is squeezed beside th' Bishop's Gate.
Father, clutching tiny hand, mother, babe in arms,
Offer Paschal praises, spiritual hymns and psalms;
William, wellknown weaver, his wife a lady's maid,
Anticipate so eagerly the Easter Day parade:
Good Rose, with deep devotion to the Passion of her Lord,
Offers God thanksgiving for the Risen Life restored.

Fleur, the fetching flower girl who resides below the Tower,
Graciously, she proffers folk a fresh and fragrant flower.
Up chirps cheerful Chandler, a City candlemaker,
Alongside *Monsieur Boulanger* the Lord Mayor's favourite baker.
'Tis rumoured, Dick with feline friend, will be the next Lord Mayor!
Hard behind, the hunchback hobbles off'ring humble prayer.
Ecstatic Clothilde capers by, flaunting Easter bonnet,
Fingering her mandolin with a joyful Easter sonnet.
There is Merlin, master mercer, up from Garlick Hill,
Beside the Austin friar scribe, quiv'ring voice and quill.

Along the ancient byways that steeply twist and bend;
Up the hill and down again, the Easter people wend
Led by Basil, Father Abbot, who joins the throng each year,
With Anna, saintly Abbess, ascetic and austere.
Behind, is Tom, *tavernier*, betrothed to Katerine:
The faithful, flock to sip Tom's brew and savour Kate's cuisine.
Look! There's Luke, th' apothecary, from Saint Bartholomew's,
If he can help a needy soul, good Luke will ne'er refuse.
Sarah, prayerful solitary, abides in Distaff Lane,
Content to sit all day a-spinning, never to complain.
Benet bargains in the chepes and at the Smithfield fayre,
Inveigling the gullible with, *"Won't you buy my ware?"*
Within the precincts of Saint Paul's, the chants reverberate:
"Exultate resurrexit" – heard e'en in Aldersgate.
Mary, ever grace-filled, like Our Lady called to pray,
Rises with the rising sun to go to Mass each day.
Eleanor, the *elegante*, - a beauty, to be sure,
Beguiles her every suitor with a most enticing lure.

Clothed in faded habit, jovial monk and gossip nun,
Exchange the cloister rigour, for the Easter morning sun.
Simon, he's a simpleton, incredibly naïve,
He sings romantic cadences, the wenches to deceive.
Helen mixes herbal cures of thyme and rosemary;
Lavender and marjoram, for a hoped-for remedy.

Watch the wily, wizened widow anxious lest she's late,
Bustling past the fisherwomen up from Billingsgate.
Mystic Margarita mingles with the crowd:
To tend the poor at Cripplegate is Margarita vowed.
She works with great compassion to help the destitute,
Begging alms from wayfarers who pass along that route.
Thence down Peter's crumbling steps they call at the Friary,
The Black Friars sing *"Laudate"* to th' Paschal Mystery.

Heads crane over windowsills to watch the passing group,
All hoping for a sprinkling from the holy water stoup.
Some fall down the creaking stairs to join the long procession,
But others have no time for prayer - they deem it *"mere obsession"*!
The lazy and the infidel, with bleary-eyes peer out,
Affronted, by the plainsong, wafting inward from without,
The infidel bestirs himself from the comfort of his slumber.
Bewildered by the singers' increasing noise and number.
Hindmost strides the mitred Bishop – he's sad that some should stray:
The absence of the slothful has caused him deep dismay.

Passing by Old Father Thames, the pilgrims turnabout
To greet the holy hermit, in his prayer so devout:
Prayer and fasting gripped him when the Forty Days began,
Londoners have now know it as the street of the Godliman.
Back to Lud they climb his hill to enter *Credo* Lane:
There to recite th' Apostles Creed, affirming Faith again.
Along the ancient alleyways closeby the muddied strand,
Here come the faithful from St Bride's to join the motley band;
Straggling into Sermon Lane, frequented by a preacher;
All held in thrall by Wyclif, controversial priest and teacher.
"Exultate resurrexit!" cries the captive crowd
Acclaiming Jesus, *"Christus"*, no longer in the shroud.
In the Paternoster Row they chant the Lord's own Prayer:
"Pater noster qui est in coelis," cuts the crisp clear air.
Then along *Ave Maria* Lane, each clasping rosary bead:
"Ave Maria, Ore pro nobis", earnestly they plead.

Through th' cathedral precincts the pilgrim souls are led;
Ended is their Act of Witness to th' Risen from the dead.

"Surrexit Dominus vere!*", in Amen Court, they cry;
"Surrexit Pastor Bonus!*",

"Amen." comes forth the firm reply.

*Taken from the medieval Latin Office.

Early 1990s

N.B. I am not aware of any historical record of an Easter celebration as related above – it's the figment of my imagination; and, with one or two exceptions, the people are fictional. However, the place names are still to be found in the City of London of today. The route the pilgrims are said to take through that part of medi-eval London is also the figment of my imagination but not beyond the realm of possibility.

SUFFERING GLORY

Almighty God, thrice holy,
We would be wholly(sic) thine,
A branch by grace engrafted
Onto the living vine.
Throb through our veins, we pray thee,
Enable us to bear
The baptism of suffering
The soul will surely share.

Lord Jesus, Blest Redeemer,
Thy Spirit we'd acquire;
The cup of suff'ring overflows
And dulls the soul's desire.
We thank God for his forgiveness,
With the hope of knowing thee;
Prepare our hearts for prayer
As in Gethsemane.

We quest the Lord in Eucharist
And from the chalice drink
The Precious Blood of Jesus Christ,
While from the Cross we shrink.
We tread the winepress, daunted:
Must it be daily trod?
The Cross repels, yet draws us nigh
To Union with God.

Unto the Crucified, we cry,
"Nail us to the Cross!
Permit thy light to shine through us
To be theotokos";
Transform us by thy saving power,
Our darkness, purify;

Impart the glory of the Cross
Our life to deify.

Oh glorious Holy Spirit,
With thee, we intercede,
Enfold us with the Love of God,
And the Spirit's gifts we need;
To incarnate thy Spirit,
The will of self efface,
Absorbing Love to render love
By God's perfecting grace,

When the cup of suffering is full,
Spilling o'er the brim,
May th' world discern God's glory
In a life poured out for Him.
Thy passion toil will then seem light,
Such is glory's weight:
That burden too is heavy,
But the privilege is great.

1995

Can be sung to: "Soul of my Saviour"

AVILA, OH AVILA!

Avila, Oh Avila!
By ancient walls surrounded,
We pilgrims come to seek your Saint
Whose sanctity abounded.

Avila, dear Avila,
Your walls provide enclosure;
Did this inspire the mystic maid
To shun the world's exposure?

Avila, spiritual Avila,
Your sturdy walls embrace her:
The Carmelite who ventured forth,
The erstwhile nun, Teresa.

2008

Some may be unaware of my devotion to St Teresa of Avila.
The above was written after a memorable pilgrimage in 2008, to Avila,
led by Father Norman Banks when he was Vicar of Mary's Church,
Walsingham, Norfolk, now Bishop of Richborough.

THE HOLY FACE

Behold, the Saviour crucified,
His Countenance divine,
Ennobled through suffering,
Compassionate, benign.

See the cruel crown of thorns,
And his penetrating eyes
Discerning sins of heart and mind:
The greed, the lust, the lies.

He loves as none has ever loved,
It is for love he dies
Heed well his deep discernment,
And the anguish in his eyes.

Respond to his perceptive gaze,
Repent and turn from sin
 Disfiguring the Holy Face,
Of the Christ, who dwells within.

Now, let us love the loveless
And smile with holy eyes:
Each person we encounter
Is Jesus in disguise.

2010

Can be sung to the tune of "Soul of my Saviour" or to the tune of "Hail to the Lord's anointed"

THRICE HOLY GOD

Sanctus, sanctus, sanctus!
Paeans of praise ascend
To the Father of the Godhead
In whom all virtues blend:
The source of love, of peace, of joy;
O, threefold Mystery,
Nourish us with *eucharist*,
And Christ's humility.
In faith we touch his garment:
The broken heart is healed;
By the Spirit's grace and power
Our discipleship is sealed.

Sanctus, sanctus, sanctus!
Sanctus is our song,
Adorning Christ our Saviour,
To whom all hearts belong.
We bear the cup of suffering
And plumb Gethsemane;
Then gaze upon the *Christus*
Whose heart bleeds on the tree.
The chalice meets our parchèd lips,
We drink and pray our part,
As we offer Christ in *eucharist*
On the altar of our heart.

Sanctus, sanctus, sanctus!
Hearts abundant sing
Uplifted by the Spirit
In threefold offering.
As love embraced our Lady,
Benedicta, in muleribus,
The Spirit comes to incarnate

The Love of God in us.
For Christ and for the Kingdom,
As disciples we enlist
With the saints, to rise in glory
At th' eternal *eucharist*.

All glory, heavenly Father,
All praise, redeeming Son,
Laudamus, Holy Spirit
In diversity you are One.

2009

Written while in respite after my legs collapsed.

CLOSE TO THE HEART OF GOD

It was at our dear Lord's behest,
I lay my head upon his breast
To hear God's heart beat firm and strong
In Love's embrace, where I belong:
Like th' belovèd disciple, I caress
Our blessèd Lord with tenderness,
Whom saints have mystically kissed
As he gives himself in Eucharist:
The offering of a pure oblation
To render us a new creation,
That we enjoin the heavenly throng
Embracing Love where we belong.
What privilege is ours to sup
With Christ who offers each the cup,
The cup of suff'ring, by joy belied,
Our wounded spirit glorified;
To die to self, to pray our part,
For love of the poor, close to his Heart,
To adore the Lord with all the blest
Who have lain their heads upon his breast.

2012

BECOMING IS BEAUTIFUL

Beautiful are you, my Love,
Altogether beautiful!
Oh my Jesus,
I pray to become
Even as you are -
Beautiful;
Perfect in your
Love
Generosity
Mercy
Forgiveness

If a worldly garment
Can offer us enhancement,
And the worldly can say,
"Your dress is most becoming!"
How much more becoming we shall be
When, by prayer and the Grace of God,
We are clothed with the Holy Spirit!
When we put on Christ.
Enrobed in the Life of his Spirit
Great will be the fulfilment of our hope that
Becoming is Beautiful

2014

AN EPIPHANY!

Lord Jesus,
I give you my heart.
As one of the 'wise' women
On the Feast of your Epiphany,
I fall down in worship,
Offering up
The tawdry treasures of my heart.
I would that I had
A heart of gold,
A spirit of pure worship,
Ever with th' fragrance of myrrh.

Holy Spirit of God,
I pray you,
Transform my heart
With a Grace of Gratitude
By love,
With love,
For love;
My heart is Christ's,
My life is His,
May God's will be done in me
An unworthy witness.

Make me an epiphany
Of the One I worship,
That the Christ in me
May show forth the glory
Of God, our Father:
I would that my life were
A true epiphany
Of Jesus Christ,
As I kneel in worship,

And lay before him
The treasures of my heart,
Now purified by grace.

All praise and thanksgiving
To the Holy Spirit
For his Real Presence within
My seeking soul:
May the Christ in me,
Glorify God
Our Father in heaven

2017

A MYSTICAL DAY

Ominous mountains encircled my life;
I floundered alone in a forest of fears;
Darkness without, depression within,
Flooded was I with interminable tears.
Praise God, Oh my soul, for my spiritual rebirth:
For gone, are the mountains of gathering gloom,
Gone, the depression that threatened all joy,
Seducing me into a chasm of doom.

Rejoice, O my soul, the suff'ring is past,
No more, th' dreaded, th' desolate Dark Night;
By Christ we're redeemed, by his Spirit we're healed,
Now I am flooded with his marvellous Light.
I thank the Lord Jesus for a spirit renewed,
His Presence restored, as I walk in his Way.
The dawn chorus greets me, as the sun meets the sky;
Prayer now blossoms like blossoming may.

I roam across pastures where paradise reigns,
Discerning God's Voice in the wafting breeze;
Enchanted, I wend through a glade of repose,
And drink in the silence 'neath the shade of the trees.
I bask in the warmth of his heavenly Love,
And bathe in a pool of his radiant Light.
I garner a bouquet of spiritual flowers;
Divine consolation brings heartfelt delight.

As dusk turns to ev'ning and the shadows grow long,
I'm aglow with the Spirit in the setting sun,
Consumed with unquenchable zeal, I abide
In love with my Saviour whose Heart I have won.
Inspired by the Spirit I glorify God,
What rapture, to joy in the bower of his Grace.
Exalted, yet humbled, by the Presence divine,
Through his wondrous Creation I gaze on his Face.

In a mystical grotto known only to God,
I hearken his voice, inviting me, "Stay!
"Contemplate Me in the depths of your soul,
As you pass the last hours of this mystical day."
I fall into 'sleep' and recline in Christ's arms,
Entranced by the Spirit's ineffable Light.
The soul's union with God, nought else can compare:
Transformed is the desert, transfigured the Night.

2015

BREAD OF ANGELS

Almighty God,
I beseech thee,
Usher me unto the heavenly Banquet
Wherein I shall behold the glory
Of the mystical Lover of my soul,
Jesus, the Christ,
Source of manna from heaven:
The Bread of Angels.

Oh Jesus, Holy Saviour,
Beloved Son of the Father,
Emmanuel, God with us,
He who came to dwell among us,
Privileged are we
That we can consume the Word of God
Written of Him in the Gospels,
The Word made Flesh;
Yet we can be consumed by Him
That sweet mystery of Love
Nascent in the sanctuary of the heart;
The soul's spiritual food:
The Bread of Angels.

Holy Spirit of God,
Clothe me
With the mantle of holiness,
That I may joyfully embrace
My belovèd Lord Jesus,
He who is our merciful Host;
Giver yet mystically given
To the great company
Of all God's saints,
Feeding them

With his eucharistic Body:
The Bread of Angels.

Holy Trinity of God,
Father, Son and Holy Spirit,
Our gracious Host
At the heavenly Banquet
Forgive me all that offends thee,
And perfect me, body, mind and spirit.
I pray thee, embrace me
Worshipping and feasting
With the saints in glory
Nourish me
With manna from heaven,
The soul's celestial food:
The Bread of Angels.

September 2018
Based on a 1980 shorter version.